Let's go by Train

Barbara Hunter

Little Nippers

Heinemann
LIBRARY

Schools Library and Information Services

www.heinemann.co.uk/library
Visit our website to find out more information about **Heinemann Library** books.

To order:
☎ Phone 44 (0) 1865 888066
▤ Send a fax to 44 (0) 1865 314091
▣ Visit the Heinemann Bookshop at www.heinemann.co.uk/library to browse our
catalogue and order online.

First published in Great Britain by Heinemann Library, Halley Court, Jordan Hill, Oxford OX2 8EJ, part of Harcourt Education. Heinemann is a registered trademark of Harcourt Education Ltd.

Editorial: Jilly Attwood and Claire Throp
Design: Jo Hinton-Malivoire and bigtop, Bicester, UK
Models made by: Jo Brooker
Picture Research: Lodestone Publishing Limited
Production: Lorraine Warner

Originated by Dot Gradations
Printed and bound in China by South China Printing Company

ISBN 978 0 431 16462 5 (hardback)
08
10 9 8 7 6 5 4 3 2

ISBN 978 0 431 16467 0 (paperback)
11 10 09
10 9 8 7 6

British Library Cataloguing in Publication Data
Hunter, Barbara
Let's go by train
385.2'2
A full catalogue record for this book is available from the British Library.

Acknowledgements
The publishers would like to thank the following for permission to reproduce photographs: Alvey and Towers p. **8-9**; Bubbles p. **7a** (John Howard), p. **18** (Jennie Woodcock); Eye Ubiquitous p. **4-5** (J. B. Pickering), **13a** (Bennett Dean); James Davis p. **20-21**; Popperfoto p. **10-11** (Michael A Nicholson); Sally and Richard Greenhill Photo Library p. **7b**; Sylvia Cordaiy Photo Library p. **16-17** (Nigel Rolstone); Tografox pp. **6**, **12**, **13b**, **14-15**, **19** (R. D. Battersby).

Cover photograph reproduced with permission of Eye Ubiquitous/J. B. Pickering.

The publishers would like to thank Annie Davy for her assistance in the preparation of this book.

Every effort has been made to contact copyright holders of any material reproduced in this book. Any omissions will be rectified in subsequent printings if notice is given to the publishers.

Contents

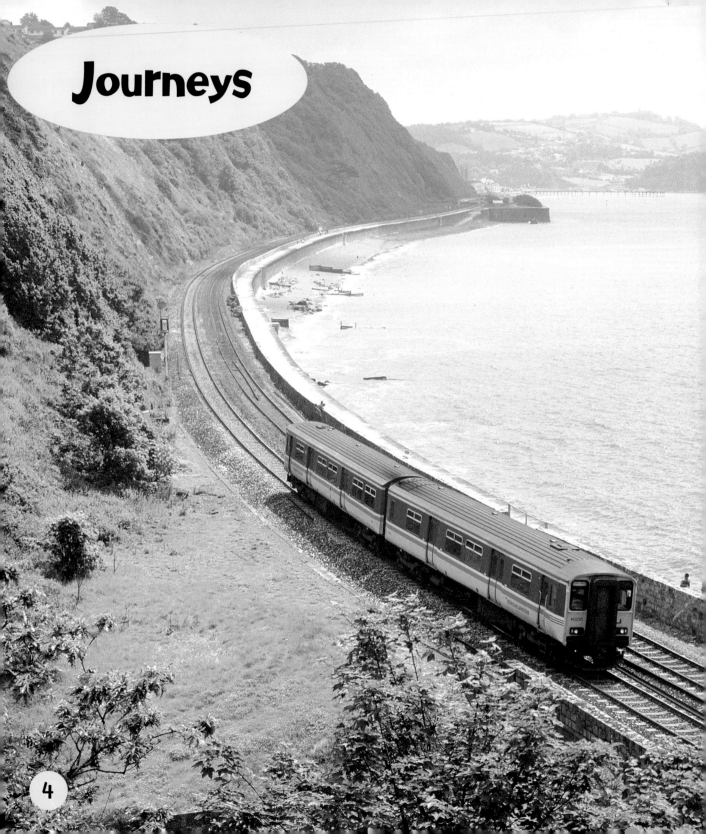

Journeys

Have you ever been
on a train journey?

Many people go by train.
They are called passengers.

Why do people go by train?

Work

Shopping

Holiday

There are places for you to sit and wait for your train.

Timetable

You need to look at a timetable to make sure you get the right train.

Tickets

You have to buy a ticket before you get onto the train.

On the platform

You wait on the platform until the train stops. Then the doors open to let you get on.

Tracks

Trains travel on tracks.

Trains can go very fast. **Zoom!**

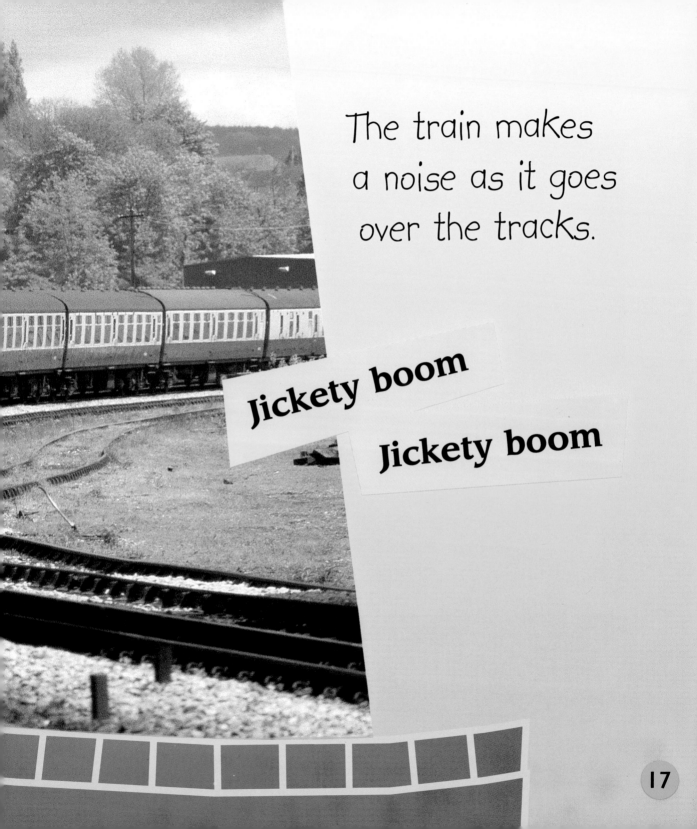

The train makes
a noise as it goes
over the tracks.

Jickety boom

Jickety boom

Passengers can often buy food and drinks on a train.

Old trains

Have you ever been on an old steam train?

Shapes

What shapes can you see on a train journey?

timetable

ticket

tracks

23

Index

The end

Notes for adults

This series supports the young child's knowledge and understanding of their world and, in particular, their mathematical development. Mathematical language like *heavy/light, long/short,* and an introduction to different shapes and positional vocabulary such as *near/far,* make this series useful in developing mathematical skills. The following Early Learning Goals are relevant to the series:
• find out about, and identify, some features of living things, objects and events that they observe
• show an awareness of similarities in shapes in the environment
• observe and use positional language.

The series explores journeys and shows four different ways of travelling and so provides opportunities to compare and contrast them. Some of the words that may be new to them in **Let's Go By Train** are *arrival, departure, timetable, tickets, platform, loud speaker, tracks, electric* and *steam trains.* Since words are used in context in the book this should enable the young child to gradually incorporate them into their own vocabulary.

The following additional information about train journeys may be of interest:
The guard blows a whistle to show that it is safe for the train to leave the station. The train runs on tracks and points change the position of the tracks. There are signals and signs by the side of the tracks that the driver has to obey in just the same way as there are rules on the road.

Follow-up activities
The child could role play situations at a train station. Areas could be set up to create a ticket office, a platform and a train. Children who have been on a train may enjoy making a record of their journey by drawing, writing or tape recording their experiences to share with others.